JOSEPH'S
DONKEY

Anthony DeStefano
Illustrated by Juliana Kolesova

SOPHIA INSTITUTE PRESS
Manchester, NH

This book is dedicated to St. Joseph, foster father of Our Lord, husband of Our Lady, head of the Holy Family, patron of a happy death, and protector of the universal Church.

—Anthony DeStefano

SOPHIA
INSTITUTE PRESS

Text Copyright © 2021 by Anthony DeStefano

Images Copyright © 2021 by Juliana Kolesova

Printed in the United States of America.

Sophia Institute Press®
Box 5284, Manchester, NH 03108
1-800-888-9344

www.SophiaInstitute.com
Sophia Institute Press® is a registered trademark of Sophia Institute.

ISBN: 978-1-64413-429-0

Library of Congress Control Number: 2021944515

First Printing, 2021

From the Bible

Joseph was a man who always did what was right.

—*Matthew 1:19 (Good News Translation)*

Behold, an angel of the Lord appeared to him in a dream, saying, "Joseph, son of David, do not fear to take Mary your wife, for that which is conceived in her is of the Holy Spirit."

—*Matthew 1:20 (RSV)*

After they had left, an angel of the Lord appeared in a dream to Joseph and said, "Herod will be looking for the child in order to kill him. So get up, take the child and his mother and escape to Egypt, and stay there until I tell you to leave." Joseph got up, took the child and his mother, and left during the night for Egypt.

—*Matthew 2:13–14 (Good News Translation)*

After three days they found him in the temple, sitting among the teachers, listening to them and asking them questions; and all who heard him were amazed at his understanding and his answers. And when they saw him they were astonished; and his mother said to him, "Son, why have you treated us so? Behold, your father and I have been looking for you anxiously." And he said to them, "How is it that you sought me? Did you not know that I must be in my Father's house?" And they did not understand the saying which he spoke to them. And he went down with them and came to Nazareth, and was obedient to them; and his mother kept all these things in her heart.

—*Luke 2:46–51 (RSV)*

Joseph was a carpenter
who lived in Galilee,
in a town called Nazareth,
a short way from the sea.

Honest, kind, and always fair,
he hardly said a word.
Work and prayer and silence
were the things that he preferred.

But Joseph's cart was filled with wood—
just loaded to the brim.
What he needed was a donkey,
big and strong like him.

So to the market Joseph went.
He looked around and saw
a dozen noisy donkeys shout:
"Hee-haw, hee-haw, hee-haw!"

But in the corner by himself
a quiet donkey stood,
looking brave and strong and silent,
like a donkey should.

Joseph saw his noble face
and loved him at first sight.
He bought the donkey on the spot
and rode him home that night.

The donkey didn't disappoint;
he did what he was told.
He worked as much as Joseph,
and his heart was good as gold.

He knew that donkeys only live
for thirty years or less.
He didn't want to waste his time
in idle laziness.

And so he worked for several months—
the best months of his life.
But nothing matched the joy he felt
when he met Joseph's wife.

Mary was a perfect girl,
graceful, pure, and sweet.
When Joseph's donkey saw her smile,
he knelt before her feet.

Joseph took him to the side
and said to him that day:
"You must protect my wife should
any danger come her way."

The donkey nodded thoughtfully
and made a silent vow:
"Although I'm very meek and shy,
I'll do my best somehow."

Soon after this, the donkey learned
the lady he adored
was pregnant with a baby boy:
Jesus Christ, the Lord.

Then from Rome came urgent news.
A census was proclaimed:
people had to travel to
the towns from which they came.

To Bethlehem the donkey went
with Mary on his back.
Joseph walked in front of them
to keep them all on track.

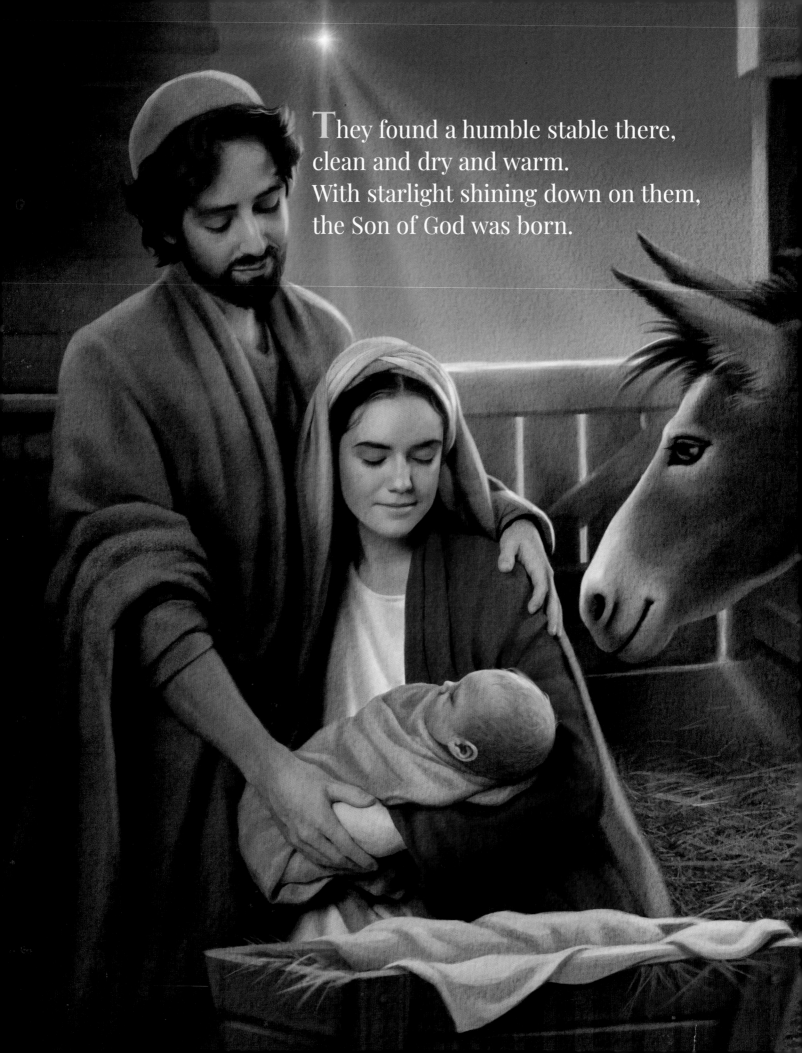

They found a humble stable there,
clean and dry and warm.
With starlight shining down on them,
the Son of God was born.

But not far off there lived a king whose jealous heart was filled with so much hatred for the Babe he tried to have Him killed.

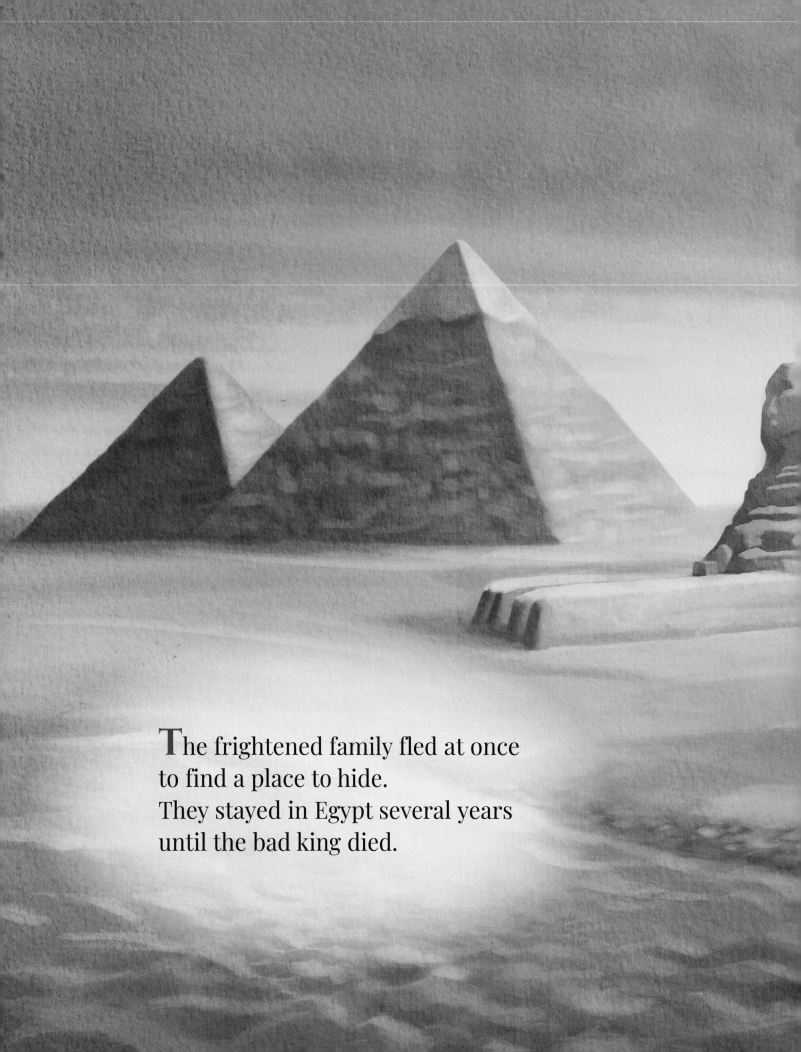

The frightened family fled at once
to find a place to hide.
They stayed in Egypt several years
until the bad king died.

Arriving home at Nazareth,
the four were safe at last.
Joseph went to work again,
and several more years passed.

The donkey worked beside him too,
hauling stones and wood,
and bearing Jesus on his back
throughout His childhood.

Jesus loved the donkey so!
He rode him every day
to places He could be alone
and close His eyes and pray.

The donkey watched the Child there,
so holy and devout.
He knew He had to be from God—
of that there was no doubt.

When the Boy was twelve years old
the family packed their things.
They journeyed to Jerusalem,
the ancient land of kings.

Jesus rode upon His friend,
and when no one could hear,
He leaned down low and whispered this
into the donkey's ear:

"A different donkey years from now
will take Me here again.
And I will suffer greatly then
but rise to life, Amen."

This secret made the donkey sad,
and tears rolled down his cheek.
He didn't show the Child, though,
or even try to speak.

They worshipped at the Temple Mount,
a wondrous sight to see.
Then they started traveling back
with all their family.

Jesus was among the crowd,
or so they thought at first.
But He was nowhere to be found,
and Joseph feared the worst.

Returning to Jerusalem
in panic and despair,
they searched three days
but couldn't find
the Child anywhere.

Just then the donkey's eyes grew wide
as if he'd seen a light.
"I know the place to look!" he thought.
"I'm sure I must be right!"

Recalling all the times he watched
the Boy alone at prayer,
he raced up to the Temple Mount
and finally found Him there!

The Boy was sitting in a group;
the sun shone on His head.
The elders of the Temple were
amazed by what He said.

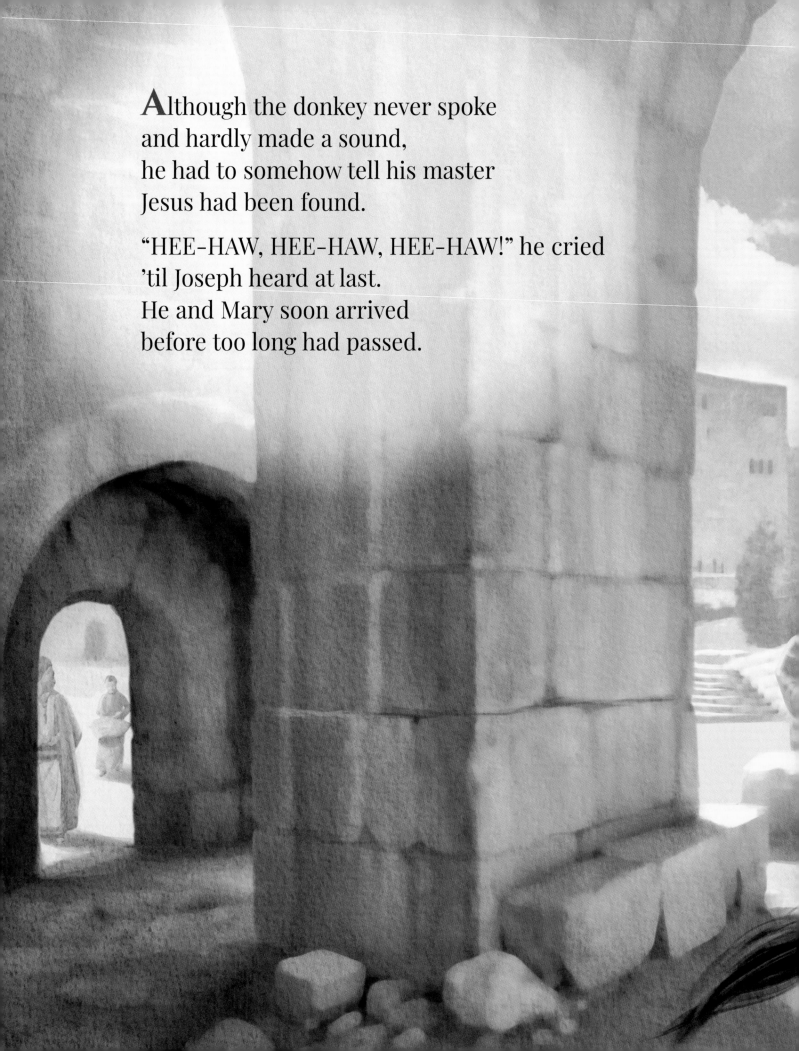

Although the donkey never spoke
and hardly made a sound,
he had to somehow tell his master
Jesus had been found.

"HEE–HAW, HEE–HAW, HEE–HAW!" he cried
'til Joseph heard at last.
He and Mary soon arrived
before too long had passed.

"Where HAVE you been?"
His parents asked,
relieved but still upset.
He answered: "In My Father's house,
Or don't you know Me yet?"

The four were glad to get back home,
the donkey most of all.
Days and months and years went by;
the little Boy grew tall.

As Jesus grew, the donkey aged;
he passed his thirtieth year.
He lost his sight, his legs got lame;
the end seemed drawing near.

He tried to limp across the field
where he had always run.
He fell three times and realized then
his walking days were done.

He carried Jesus many years
when Jesus was a child.
Now Jesus carried HIM back home
so he could rest awhile.

Jesus sighed and said to him:
"I know it's getting dark.
You've finished your great mission,
and on Mine I'll soon embark."

Mary rubbed the donkey's neck
and kissed him on his head.
She gave him something cold to drink
and offered him some bread.

Joseph sat by his old friend
and whispered lovingly:
"I've been your master many years,
but now I set you free.
When you arrive at Heaven's gate,
please wait awhile for me.
I'm growing very old myself
and won't be long, you'll see."

Then Jesus looked at him and said:
"My arms and hands take hold.
O good and faithful servant,
fear not the dark or cold.
For in My Father's Kingdom
are fields of green and gold,
with miles and miles to run in,
and happiness untold.
Just close your eyes now gently.
Be faithful and be bold.
Open them again now,
and then My friend…